CHEEP LAUGHS

1025 REALLY DAFT GAGS

CHEEP LAUGHS

1025 REALLY DAFT GAGS

BY THE UK PUN CHAMPION
DARREN WALSH

CENTURY

Published by Century 2014

2 4 6 8 10 9 7 5 3 1

First published in Great Britain in 2014 by
Century
Random House, 20 Vauxhall Bridge Road,
London SW1V 2SA

www.randomhouse.co.uk

Addresses for companies within
The Random House Group Limited can be found at:
www.randomhouse.co.uk

The Random House Group Limited Reg. No. 954009

A CIP catalogue record for this book
is available from the British Library

ISBN 9781780893778

Penguin Random House is committed to a sustainable future for
Our business, our readers and our planet. This book is made from
Forest Stewardship Council® certified paper.

MIX
Paper from
responsible sources
FSC® C018179

Printed and bound in Great Britain by Clays Ltd, St Ives Plc

DEDICATION

To my family, friends, comedy chums
and pun-suffering girlfriend.

FOREWORD

When I was first asked to make this book I thought, 'that's novel' as up until now, my jokes were only popular with butterflies (word of moth). I was going to ask a random girl to write this, but then I thought that might be a bit foreword. I'm also hoping to win an art prize for flicking through it really quickly (the Turner Prize).

Forewords you don't want to hear before reading this book:

'Translated into ancient Greek'
'Printed with invisible ink'
'Punchlines are not included'.

This joke book encompasses four years of writing puns and drawings on the comedy circuit. It is best enjoyed in manageable chunks. Do not attempt to read it all in one go or your brain will cave in. Also, make sure you don't turn it round the wrong way or you won't see the funny side.

Big thanks go to asasdasdasdasd.

Darren Walsh
London
2014

THE JOKES

1

Man walks into a tavern . . . Oh you won't get it, it's an Inn joke.

2

Someone offered me a loud stereo, but I turned it down.

3

I'm going to Israel, but don't Tell Aviv.

WHERE'S MY CHANGE?!

TIGHT NIT

4

Went out last night and woke up with a pound coin shoved up my arse. I must have been trolleyed.

5

I just deleted all the German names off my phone. It's Hans free.

6

My workmates think I'm an alcoholic. I'm wasted in this job.

7

Bilbo Baggins is starring in a new film about a gang of German terrorists who take over a skyscraper. *Old Hobbits Die Hard.*

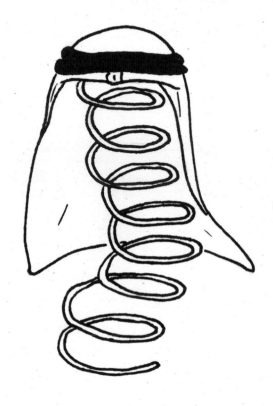

ARAB SPRING

8

I've got a friend who's obsessed with completing his Beatles collection. He needs *Help.*

ASS SEEN ON TV

9

Went to my allotment and found that there was twice as much soil as there had been the week before. The plot thickens.

10

I refuse to eat kebabs unless
they've been flown in specially by
my personal gourmet kebab chef.
I'm a Prima Doner.

11

There's only one way to raid a
bakery: all buns glazing.

12

I hate people who play low
frequency guitars. I'm bassist.

13

Last night I dreamt I was drowning
in vodka. Absolut nightmare.

14

My dad keeps leaving his car in my driveway. He's got Parkinson's.

15

I was going to write a comedy sketch about a chicken coup that turns into a pub, but I'm not going to put all my eggs in one bar skit.

16

There seems to be arise in knighthoods.

17

My cat is recovering from a massive stroke.

18

Meanderthal: an extinct human species that wanders around aimlessly.

19

I've just been diagnosed with kleptomania. My psychiatrist said that if I need anything, her door is always open.

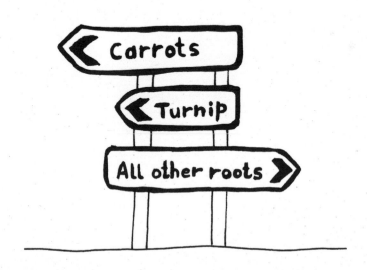

CROSSWORD

20

I phoned the Seaworld dolphin
show centre, and they said 'calls
would be recorded for training
porpoises'. So THAT'S how they
do it.

BUTTERFLY

21

I wear platform shoes, but I take
them off once I'm on the train.

22

Don't bother having a mint-sucking
competition with a dyslexic – they
use dirty tic tacs.

23

There's a new German perfume
that dries really quickly.
It's called Coco Schnell.

24

An Irish man asked me which
character he should play in the
nativity play. I said be Jesus.

25

'My nephew would like to borrow
your *Toy Story* costume.'
'Oh Woody?'

DOG POUND

26

A bunch of Morris dancers asked me to go canal boating with them. I said, 'I wouldn't touch your barge with a maypole.'

27

Post traumatic stress: sending someone anthrax.

28

My mate challenged me to a donkey race, but he got disqualified for a false start. I kicked his ass.

29

The Addams Family gave me a severed hand, but it's not really my Thing.

30

'Woop, woop' – it's da sound of da police.
'Uncle Darren, Uncle Darren' – it's da sound of my niece.

31

The study of white blood cells isn't exactly the same as red blood cells, but it's in a similar vein.

32

Went to a nightclub that was full of orcs, beasts and trolls. It was Mordor on the dance floor.

33

Turned up drunk to a party dressed as an OXO cube. I was the laughing stock.

GORILLA MARKETING

RISTMASCH
ISTMASCHR
STMASCHRI
TMASCHRIS
MASCHRIST
ASCHRISTM
SCHRISTMA
CHRISTMAS
That's Christmas sorted.

35

Just read an article in a trashy magazine about 'The Top 10 Turn-Offs for Women'. Apparently the biggest one is Junction 4 on the M11.

36

Got a free chimney the other day. It was on the house.

Saw this bloke at a bus stop that said 'Out of use' on it.

'What are you waiting for?' I asked

'A giant shrimp is coming to pick me up in exactly 60 seconds,' he said. 'And . . . if I miss that, another giant shrimp is going to pick me up exactly 60 seconds later . . .'

'Of course,' I said.

Ha! One prawn every minute . . .

CHARACTER WITNESS

38

If I take my cat to the vet, he dies.
If I take him home, he dies.
Cat's 22.

39

All my family has diarrhoea. It runs
in the genes.

40

Superficial people are sooo last
year.

41

So, apparently I'm not good at
expressing myself. Can't say I'm
surprised.

42

I was going to kill a wasp, but I bottled it.

43

I'm a borderline racist. I hate borderlines. They can go back to their own two countries.

44

Squeezed myself into someone's house through a cat flap. I thought, what have I let myself in for?

45

My mother used to say, '. . . and if Garry Kasparov jumped off a cliff would you follow him?'
I thought, that old chess nut.

46
K e v i n ← Kevin Spacey.

47
How do evil cows laugh?
Moo-hahahaha.

48
A tourist on the London Underground asked, 'Could you tell me how to get to the airport via Barking?' So I pointed at a map and woofed.

49
What do you get if you remove an L and an I from 'oblivious'?
The answer is obvious.

MAGNUM PI

FORENSICS

50
Everyone's dressing up as East-End gangsters. It's all the Krays.

51
When the Duchess of Cambridge went into labour, Prince William's heir started falling out.

52

I received some bad news whilst eating a curry at an Indian restaurant. My naan had slipped into a korma.

53

ygolohcysp ← Reverse psychology.

54

Did you know that raincoats are made in Iran? An' Iraq.

55

This girl is dating me because I'm a surgeon. I think she's just using me forceps.

56
Green men make me cross.

57
I can impersonate a baby deer with either my right or left hand. I'm bambidextrous.

BACK CATALOGUE

58
I got stopped in the street and asked if I could hyphenate two words. Made a dash for it.

59

You shouldn't mix business
with pleasure, because you get
bpulseianseusrse.

60

If Catwoman decided to go to
Nepal, what would Catman do?

61

'Where the sheeps have no
naaaame.' 'Ewe 2.'

62

My school are saying I'm not fit
to teach Satanism anymore.
Unbelievable. After all those
sacrifices I made.

63

Young men are pretending that they fancy their mother in order to claim welfare from the government. It's benefit Freud.

64

Phoned my insurance company for a quote. They just said, 'Live as if you were to die tomorrow. Learn as if you were to live for ever.' – Mahatma Gandhi.

65

I turned my mate's joke book the wrong way round. He didn't see the funny side.

66
Magπum ← Magnum Pl.

67
What good is making a website about 'stranger danger' if there's a pop up saying 'Accept cookies'?

68
I tried to convert a hen to Christianity, but chicken doubt.

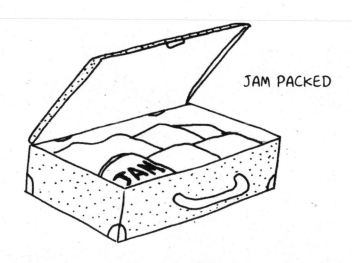

JAM PACKED

WESTERN-SUPER-MARE

69

I heard a sneeze from the chimney. I think Santa's coming down with something.

70

Went out drinking last night and woke up in a house that wasn't my own. Cos I'm still renting.

71

My friend is sexually attracted to seaweed. I think he should sea kelp.

72

My friend says I just forward emails on without reading them properly. I resent that.

73

Lost my wallet in the sliced
bread section of the bakery. Went
through thick and thin getting it
back.

74

An overweight shop assistant
said I couldn't have a refund as my
shirt had stretched 'naturally'. I
think she was trying it on.

75

Got drunk, went dancing, came
home and told my son that he
wasn't getting any inheritance. I
really let my heir down.

76

Since leaving Camelot, the knights are lonely.

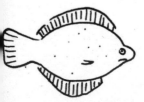  

FIND A HAPPY PLAICE

77

Went psychic speed-dating. Every woman I met was a grumpy clairvoyant. I thought, I've got to find a happy medium here somewhere.

78

Someone stole my *Miami Vice* duvet set. Police are on the case.

TEDDY BUOY

79

Did a gig on a donkey. Died on my ass.

80

I was drinking my life away when the hotel reception rang. It was a real wake-up call.

81

Petit pois. There, I've said my peas.

82

I suppose I shouldn't force American schoolkids to use the word 'headmaster', but it's the principle.

83

Another cheap jack-in-the-box that doesn't work properly. No surprise there.

84

My friend keeps setting fire to Belgian detectives. He's a Poirotmaniac.

85

I use a block of cheese as an alarm clock. I wake up when it goes off.

86

Posh heroin addicts tend to get Pimm's and needles.

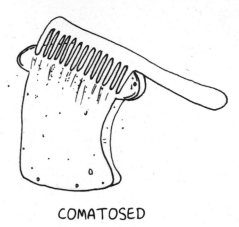

COMATOSED

87

A ninja has challenged me to a fight, but I'm not shuriken make it.

88

It's nice being a giant, but I think I've got an obsessed fan. She's beanstalking me.

MAN EATING PLANT

89

My friend says he was the original author of *War and Peace*. Sounds like a Tolstoy to me.

90

A donkey ate my window. That's a pane in the ass.

91

I asked someone from Birmingham which one was the Slough train. Been on here bloody ages.

92

I asked the barman where the toilet was. He replied, 'Use your instincts.' I said, 'I'll follow my nose then, cos your inn stinks.'

93

Bloody warrior princesses, coming over here and stealing our jobs. Sorry, I'm Xenaphobic.

94

Slipped and fell into a purple shrub. I'll have to be more careful in fuchsia.

BLIND DRUNK

95

My girlfriend keeps asking me the time, precisely to the nearest 60th of a minute. I think she's using me for secs.

WHIPLASH

96

Oktoberfest brings out the wurst in people.

97

Told a guy he looked like Che Guevara. He told me I looked like Che Guevara. Two Che.

98

I heard this from someone: late at night, butterflies go round the city streets mugging people with light-bulbs. It must be an urban moth.

99

A convent have just hired the A-Team. I love it when some nuns plan together.

HE'S GETTING ON A BIT...

100

My mate has bought a silencer for his gun. He kept that quiet.

101

I hired a wizard, but he turned up without his magic stick. Can't get the staff these days.

STREETHAWK

102

My friend Andrew has shortened
his name. That's Andy.

103

Went to a psychiatrist's fancy-
dress party as Gloria Gaynor. At
first I was a Freud . . .

104

I reversed into a purple shrub at
exactly 88 miles per hour. Back to
the fuchsia.

105

The zoo have put a fridge in the
monkey enclosure! Cool bananas.

107

Someone went and cleaned out my drainpipes whilst I was on holiday. Gutted.

108

My niece asked me what age discrimination meant. I told her she was too young to understand.

109

Have you heard the rumours about a new revolving skyscraper? There's a few stories going round.

110

My friend slept with the revenue inspector to avoid paying tax. That's gross.

PUBLIC HOUSE

110

U2 have started using razor blades instead of plectrums. It's cutting edge.

111

I won a year's supply of ice cream, but there was a wafer in the contract.

APERITIF

112

I never thought in a million years that I would be able to build a jack-in-the-box. I surprise myself sometimes.

113

Hoovers suck.

114

A fairground attendant said I was too tall to go on his ride. I thought he was just being tallist, but then I realised I was tallest.

115

Don't try to make an anagram of the word 'stardies'. It spells disaster.

116

I had an operation to convert me into a duck. I was left with a huge bill.

117

I've been told I'm a crap shepherd, but I'm not not gonna lose sheep over it.

118

Went on a date with a gym instructor. Didn't work out.

THE 'YOLKS' ON YOU

PUNGENT

119

My mate reckons all dogs in the army are good for nothing but cleaning floors. That's a sweeping General Alsatian.

120

I opened the wrong safe. It wasn't my vault.

121

If you like to have a laugh in a lobby, I've got a joke foyer.

122

I was going to start up a bland indie piano-rock band, but in the end I decided I wasn't Keane.

123

I told Evan I was miserable. Evan knows I'm miserable now.

124

I went to the dentist and asked for the cheapest possible fillings. I left with a mouthful of baked beans and tuna mayo (with sweetcorn).

125

My mate has slept with over 100 poets. He's riddled.

126

Tried to change a one pound coin into American currency. It made no cents.

127

People say my dentist is a bit of a Nazi, but that couldn't be Führer from the tooth.

WHAT'S THAT SUPPOSED TO MEAN!?

SHORT FUSE

128

My friend is trying to set me up with a North American rodent, but she's not normally the type I gopher.

129

If a doe wants to celebrate her last night before getting married, what does the stag do?

ANDY MAORI

130

I asked the executioner if he fancied another pint, but he had to head off.

CHEAPSKATE

131

I made some pasta for the son of Zeus. It was Apollognese.

132

I'm really good at making malt tea. I'm malt tea talented.

MOSQUITO

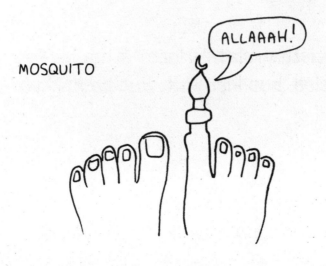

133
I removed my doorbell. It had a knock-on effect.

134
I love magnesium, it's amazinc.

135
My tandem skydiving instructor and I have had a massive falling out.

136

I ended a relationship with a blow-up doll, but I let her down gently.

137

My computer wouldn't let me use the word 'luggage' as a password. It was case sensitive.

138

I tried to watch a YouTube video of a car being polished, but it kept buffering.

139

People who don't punctuate their sentences They should put a stop to it.

140

I told the police I was purchasing herbs for cooking, but I was just buying myself some thyme . . .

141

Every time I eat beetroot, a little part of me dyes.

142

I ate at a restaurant called 'Set up, Punchline'. The service was a joke.

143

I castrated a sheep. That's raised the baa.

144

My friend is an ice cream man during the day, a dominator at night. He calls himself Mr Whippy.

145

Jo/y ← Joy Division.

LOYALTY CARD

146

Someone called Tetris followed me on Twitter. I blocked him.

147

My next gig is in a Weight Watchers class. I'm trying to reach a bigger audience.

148

They're making a documentary about a cure for arthritis. It's called *Silence of the Limbs*.

149

I bought my ex-girlfriend an e-book. I thought it would rekindle our relationship.

150

Went on a date dressed as an overturned traffic cone. Got stood up.

HOOVER DAM

151

I got reviewed by camouflaged insects. They were really harsh crickets.

152

I decided to eat a curry halfway through a marathon. It was a bad decision in the long run.

HANDBRAKE

153

NASA have reported a suspicious bag on one of their rockets. A case is being launched.

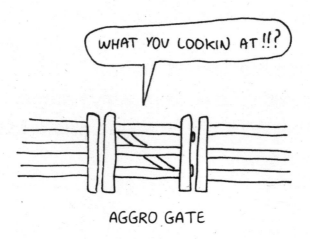

WHAT YOU LOOKIN AT!!?

AGGRO GATE

154

I haven't actually heard anyone say I'm paranoid, but I know they're thinking it.

155

Worst auntie of all time ever? Auntie Climax.

156

I used the self-checkout at the supermarket. Turns out I'm fine.

157

My friend keeps bowing to peer pressure to wear a size 8 dress. I don't think she should, she's bigger than that.

158

In a desperate attempt to find money, Greece is selling fake cement to neighbouring islands. They're going to con Crete.

159

I don't believe in infection. I'm septic.

160

Palestine sent a stripper to the United Nations conference. It was a sassy nation attempt.

161

This Scottish guy was like, 'but hoo will ah knoa when ya email her?' I said, 'I'll CC you, Jimmy.'

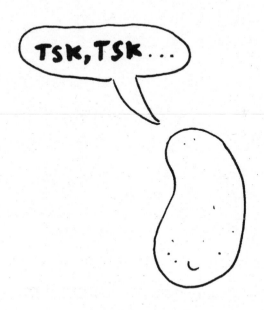

TUSCAN BEAN

162

A woman has been using my underground waste system. I'm gonna sewer.

THE DOOR'S AJAR

163

It's a bit depressing having a luminous foot, but at least there's light at the end of the toenail.

164

We left our baby on a doorstep.
He's self-raising.

165

Alloy Vera: what we called our gran
after she had her hip replacement.

166

I was driving around looking for a
doctor's surgery, but my sat-nav
didn't have GPs.

167

Went for a job interview dressed as
Lassie, but apparently I was too
collified.

SMART CASUAL RACIST

168

Asked the man at KFC if he could make sure there were 2 burgers in my bun. 'Of course!' he shouted. 'OK,' I said. 'Just double chicken.'

169

My girlfriend and I were arguing over who should get the best storage space, so we drew lots. I got the shorts drawer.

170

It's rare to see a well-done steak.

171

Took a girl on a date to a coconut shy. We hit it off straight away.

172

Time to give my snooker cue a rest.

173

I asked for some Thai food in a Vietnamese restaurant. Phở pas.

174

Cagin' chicken isn't free range.

175

I went to a Satanists' fancy dress party as a lamb. Got totally slaughtered.

176

You look like my late aunt. She's not here yet.

177

Saw a ham salad bap and a deer playing chess. It was a roll playing game.

178

I'm to guest star in an episode of *The Simpsons*. I didn't plan it, I just got drawn in.

ROLAND RAT

179

My dog isn't sure whether he's broccoli or not. He's a border cauliflower.

180

Einstein used to work out a lot.

SCHEDULE

181

Did a gig for a blind charity. I thought it would be funny to do the whole thing in braille, but the crowd weren't feeling it.

182

'Hello, Fishermen's Advice Bureau?'
'Help! I've got a bite, what do I do?!'
'Please hold the line . . .'

183

'My hair colour makes me look fat.'
'Well, why don't you diet?'

184

2 sheep in a strip club.
One says, 'How did we end up in here?'
Other says, 'I was following ewe . . .'

185

I was in a band called The Tablecloths, but I left because we only did covers at weddings.

186

Don't believe everything you hear about skyscrapers. There's 2 sides to every storey.

187

When I was a lecturer at the Warner Brothers Studios, I taught 'I saw a puddy tat'.

188

My wrestling partner said, 'Look . . . I think I've got a sweat rash in the shape of you.' I said, 'We need to talc.'

THICK HEAD OF HARE

MASSIVE HEAD RUSH

189

When I was at college, I let a bunch of alchemy students experiment on me. I was easily lead.

190

Black sambuca: it's not really liqueur, but it's liqueur-ish.

191

I bumped into Lancelot at the pub. He was holding a luminous pen. It was the highlight of the knight.

192

My girlfriend and I keep breaking up and getting back together.
She's made out of Lego.

193

On holiday in Sri Lanka, I got stuck in Columbo Airport customs for hours! They kept saying: 'Just one more thing . . .'

194

R. Kelly. I believe I can touch this guy.

HEY MATE, CAN I STAY AT YOURS TONIGHT?

CAR CRASH

195

Took a girl on a date up the Statue
of Liberty, but on the way down
we got completely lost and had a
massive argument. Must've got off
on the wrong foot.

196

Twas the night before Christmas,
when all through the house.
Not a creature was stirring, not
even a mouse.
Last time I hire animals to do the
cooking.

POSITION

NERVOUS

NERVOUS DISPOSITION

197

There's a new horror film out based on the antics of Jesus and His disciples. It's called *I Know What You Did Last Supper.*

MOULDY

198

I was going to do stand-up comedy on a horse and cart, but the gig got pulled.

199

I hired Death to decorate my living room. Didn't think of reaper cushions.

MEER TRIFLE

200

I won a pumpkin-carving contest against a class of 8-year-olds.
It was a hollow victory.

201

I never read the IKEA instruction manuals. I don't believe in shelf help books.

202

What do you call a Dutch man with a gerbil up his bottom? Hamster Dan.

203

I've been promised a smelly fart, but I'm not holding my breath.

204

I'm trying to memorise all the James Bond films starting from the most recent, but it's not easy to *No*.

205

I only ever use one type of wood. I'm a mahoganist.

206

I have a lot of die-hard fans. They're not here tonight though, they're at home watching *Die Hard II*.

207

My pet snail has started talking to me. He's really come out of his shell.

208

My doctor says I'm not eating enough pheasant. I need to up my game.

209

Will Smith is set to star in the new *CSI: Bel Air*. He'll be looking for fresh prints.

MEN'S ELF

210

It was horrible having a broken neck, but now I can look back and laugh.

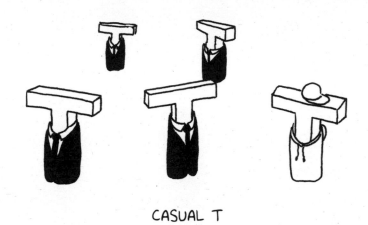

CASUAL T

211

I watched an advert for dog food that had a frame rate of 25fps with dimensions of 720 x 576. It was PAL.

212

I ordered the nettle tea thinking it'd be cheap. Got stung.

213

For breakfast, my mum would squat over a piece of toast and give birth to an orange. That's what my mama laid.

214

'Is that a gate?'
'No, a fence.'
'None taken: Is that a gate?'

215

Someone told me I looked like Gary Barlow. I'm not sure how I should take that.

216

I got facial hair all of a sudden. Just a beard from nowhere.

217

The Genie said, 'Right, that's it! No more wishes for anyone.'
Someone must've rubbed him up the wrong way.

218

This cat dressed as a hen winked at me. She was chicken meow.

219

The Mayan calendar predicted humankind would get a licking from South American llamas. It's the second coming of the alpaca lips.

220

I made up my bed this morning. There isn't one.

BATTERED COD

221

This bloke told me he needed more time to decide whether he was a Communist or not. I think he was Stalin.

222

I play grade 4 piano. It makes the grade 8 students jealous.

223

A pig knocked on my door dressed as a ghost. What a frightful boar.

BUFFALO
MOZZARELLA

224

'Do unto terrapins as you would do unto turtles.'
That's what Jesus tortoise.

225

In an effort to ease the Eurozone crisis, Turkey will now be baste in Greece.

226

'Officer, I'm giving myself up. I have weed on me.'
'Yes, I can see it ran down your leg.'

227

An oxymoron graduate undergoing supervised training? That's a contradiction interns.

228
I'm terrible at abbreviating words.
Take the word egg, for example.

229
Anyone know the latest Polynesian
Football League scores? Last time
I checked it was Hawaii 5-0.

230
Va der
Vad er
V ader
Vade r
Space in Vaders.

231
I entered a television repair
competition, but it was fixed.

AVIS have claimed they are best car rental company. The Truth? Hertz.

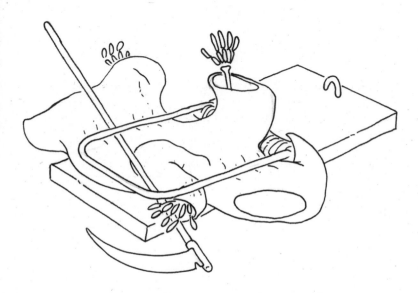

DEATH TRAP

233

New research shows that a Venus fly trap can take a man's head off. I think they're looking into it a bit too much.

234

Saw a man with no arms or legs climb up a plank of wood. It was nail-biting.

CUPBOARD

235

I got my old job back as a puncture repair man. I feel hole again.

236

You shouldn't eat wooden shoes from Holland. Clogs up your digestive system.

BOYZ IN DA HOOD

237

Jay-Z was moaning that his remote car fob had broken. I said, 'Alicia Keys work, mate.'

238

Some asked me for some PG Tips. I said *Back to the Future* was good.

239

I left a fish in between the encyclopaedias at the library. Hopefully that'll secure my plaice in the history books.

240

Saw a film about indigestion called *Pepto*. It was a bismol.

241

What do you call three members of ABBA in a French slaughterhouse? ABBA Trois.

242

Broken tripods. Can't stand them.

FULL STOP

HUGE FOLLOW WING

243

First day in my new job as an escape artist. I'm really struggling.

244

Went for a quick drink after work with a fertilised egg. One turned into two, two turned into four . . .

245

I work part-time at a hairdressers for insects. They've asked me to go perm an ant.

246

I'm watching a Blu-ray DVD about a ham sandwich. It's been digitally remustard.

247

I HATE SPRING WATER. There I said it. Better to get these things out rather than bottling it up.

248

I was going to click the Favourites button, but it's a bit too close to Home.

FAMOUS

249

I'm going Thailand to learn boxing. Mustn't forget my jabs.

250

Got really depressed after I lost my sat-nav. I didn't know where to turn.

251

The doctor told me I have a diagonal nose. I've been diagnosed.

252

My girlfriend wrote 'Shouldn't you have proposed to me by now?' on a balloon, so I popped the question.

a rinkd
a inkdr
a nkdri
a kdrin
a drink
Looks like a drink is in order.

PIPE DREAM

254

Dated an astronomy student, but I couldn't give her the space she wanted.

255

I come from Kerplunk. No one visits me 'cos it's in the sticks.

256

Sean Connery won't let anyone else wear his shrimp costume. He's shellfish.

257

I was looking for the train when I saw a sign that said 'station close', so I thought, can't be that far.

258

The bouncer said I couldn't get in.
Technical issues apparently.
'Technical issues?' I said. 'What
technical issues?'
He then pointed at my fluorescent
trainers. 'No, mate. No technicolour
shoes.'

259

To the guy who wrote 'knobhea' on
my wall. Complete knobhead.

260

My mate is staying in tonight
and dressing up as Super Mario,
chasing green mushrooms around
the flat. Some people need to get
a life.

261

Eastern European required.
Position now filled.
The Czech is in the post.

YOU ONLY WON BECAUSE YOU HAVE A MORE EXPENSIVE TENNIS RACKET

SOUR GRAPES

262

Picked my jacket up from the
Chinese dry cleaners at 3pm, but
it had 5pm stitched into it. It was
a different time sewn.

263

m+e. That sums me up.

264

A chicken has been banished from a coop after growing too large. It was ostrich-sized.

PEOPLE WATCHING

265

Read a touching autobiography about a battery hen that became a free-range chicken. It's called *The Secret of My Six Eggs*.

266

A knight bus leans to one side. It slants a lot.

THE SHORT SHARK REDEMPTION

267

I did a 1-inch punch the other day. Turned out I massively underestimated how many guests were coming to my cocktail party.

268

I don't know how battery hens coop.

269

New government legislation: a crackdown on faulty fertility clocks. They hope it will encourage women to buy a logical clock.

270

I'd vote for the Tory Party in Somerset, but I wouldn't in Dorset.

271

Went to see Mick Hucknall about
my shoulder feeling tight.
He said, 'What about your knee?'
M'knee's too tight to mention.

272

Someone wrote 'bum' on my
forehead whilst I was asleep. Now
every time I look in the mirror, my
name is mud.

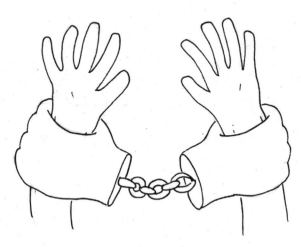

FISTY CUFFS

273

Marcel Marceau and Étienne Decroux both came up with the 'pulling rope' trick at the same time. Great mimes think alike.

LAYING OFF THE BOOZE

274

Last Internet date I go on. 'Shy and retiring' it said. She was 59 and quiet.

275

My friend has started typing in capitals. Why the shift?

276

Got sacked for moisturising too much at work. On my way out they said, 'Don't forget to pick up your E45.'

277

'You've been reading *Huckleberry Finn* again haven't you?'
'Yes, how did you know?'
'Cos Tom Sawyer.'

278

My Scottish father left me a potato farm. My reputation is in tatties.

279

People in Alaska shop like there's snow tomorrow.

280

This* Horse
God of This*
Lords of This*
World This* II
This* and Peace
This* of the Worlds
(*This means war)

281

I went into WH Smith and saw a sign saying 'Free water with the *Daily Telegraph*.' So I rolled up the *Telegraph* as tightly as I could and pierced a hole in the bottle.

282

The people renting my house drink super-strong low-budget lager, but they're super tenants.

283

Doctors have given me a telephone box to help me control my anger, but it's taking a while to kick in.

284

C

 a

  l

   v

Calv incline.

TRIUMPH

UMPH...

PIG STY

285

Someone in the office asked if anyone had a contacts solution. I suggested an address book.

286

I always knew my comedy career would have me filling stadiums. Just got a job driving a digger.

287

I thought I'd run out of haemorrhoid pills, but then I realised I had piles.

288

I deposited a bright light in a bank account. Got 6 moths' interest.

289

Why did ABBA get hungry for spicy chicken? Because they heard the bell for Nando's.

FOUR POSTER BED

290

I thought I saw a bunch of people getting drunk around a dead body, but it was awake.

291

My abseiling instructor started shouting abuse at me, but I'm not gonna lower myself.

292

Went to an international conference of world leaders. Can't remember what it was called, the G8 . . . summat or other.

293

There should be a dentist called Clean Matifah.

294

My art director asked me to use a clean font, so I used Arial.

295

Our therapy session was in a monastery this week. I found it hard to talk at first, but then realised we were a monk's friends.

296
Went to a David Hasselhoff convention, but only stayed for the first Hoff.

297
My mate's folks own a sauna. He's always sponging off his parents.

298
I'm going to a fancy dress party as a medium-sized cardboard box. I cannot contain myself.

SAD CASE

299

'Is it wee you're looking for?' –
Urinal Richie.

WIFI

300

I was worried about making this
joke self-referential, but no meta.

301

As my flatmate handed me the
rice-strainer, I told him I was really
tired from cooking all day, and that
he should just put his feet up. I'm
pass sieve aggressive.

302

Was a bit lonely, so I put my face on a Wild West poster and stuck it on a lamp post. Now I feel wanted.

303

My girlfriend said that the red doorbell I bought her isn't very environmentally friendly.
I might buy 'er da grey doorbell.

304

Went for a drink with a circle. Kept saying, 'your round.' Really winds him up.

305

I deposited money in a Greek bank account. My investment is in ruins.

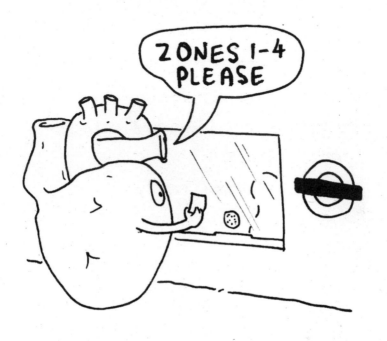

HEART BUY PASS

BAY LEAF

306
Thought I had tickets for the upper circle, but turned out it was the stalls. Reduced me two tiers.

307
Turns out Bing Crosby was in the mafia! That was pretty bada Bing.

308

So you've loaded an image of a
donkey and don't know how to save
it?
File > Save Ass.

309

When my flatmates go out, I wear
their clothes and pretend to be
a dinosaur. Tonight I might try
Sarah's tops.

310

You'd think putting some money
into a homeless man's open bottle
of suncream would be a nice thing
to do, but it was lost in tramp's
lotion.

311

Someone tried to kill themself by building a long ramp going into a drain. It was an attempted sewer slide.

312

Fat children are controlled by their sofas. Child obey settee.

313

I used to hate audiences who didn't appreciate puns, but they've groan on me.

314

Saw a box of eggs in the supermarket that said '£995.' Then I realised it just said 'Eggs.'

315

When I was a boy I had a gambling problem. I remember at the poker table, this man said, 'I'll raise you.' . . . And that's how I was adopted.

316

I might have got a job mixing cement, but nothing concrete as yet.

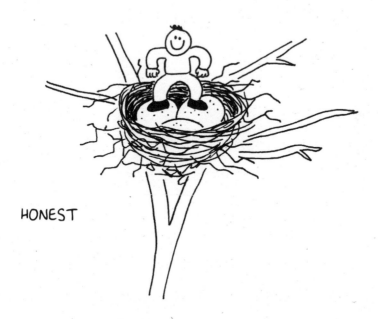

HONEST

317

People who quote me without correcting my spelling make me [sic].

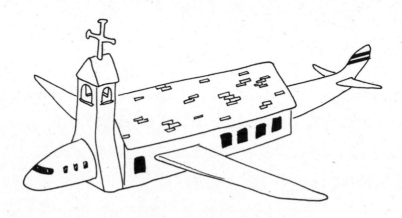

LONG HALL FLIGHT

318

My friend has trouble squeezing Indian snack food in his tiny lunch box, but he makes samosa fit.

319

I ♥ bypass surgery.

320

Went to a nightclub in France and pooed myself. It was merde on the dance floor.

321

My fiancée said, 'I hope you put as much effort into our honeymoon as you did that stag do.' So after the wedding, I took her to Prague and we walked around in the freezing cold for 4 hours looking for a strip club.

322

My mate Paul asked me how to become a great leader and inspire others. I said, 'Sit an exam, Paul.'

323

It wasn't till Linda married Paul McCartney that I knew who she was. I hadn't heard of herbivore.

324

This woman just told me she was pregnant with her first child. That's disgusting.

325

ABBA made me a monk curry. My tikka chants on me.

326

The World's tallest man competition is now solely being decided by Miss World. That's pretty judge men tall.

327

My friend has just written a book about himself, but he doesn't have a front cover. He ought to buy a graphic.

328

People tell me I should stop complaining about Australian wine, but I have no gripes.

329

I took a tour with 3 pigs around the cities of Italy. First pig showed me Milan, second pig showed me Rome, but the third pig just said, 'Alright, lads, we're going to a floating city with loads of fit Italian birds in it.'
That was the 'show Venice' pig.

330

Princess Diana's family wanted everyone at her funeral to wear 'smart casual.' Bloody Marxist Spencers.

331

I love purchasing bears from the Arctic. Argh! I hate purchasing bears from the Arctic. I'm buy-polar.

HELLO SAILOR...

BOOT CAMP

332

This guy at work keeps dressing up as a cashew. He's office nut.

333

Having an irrational fear of baby sheep. Is lamb a phobia?

334

Jew-ish: slightly Jewish.

MOCK THE WEEK

335

Dogs make more scents than cats.

336

Lack-toes intolerance: fear of stumpy feet.

337

Went on a date with a retractable pen. We just clicked.

338

Tried to make a cloth laugh last night. Had a vague impression of Jesus stained on it . . . Didn't smile once, just stared at me. Tough shroud.

339

Buy air freshener from Lidl. It's common scents.

340

My currant girlfriend just dumped me. I guess everything happens for a raisin.

341

Just got beaten up by a deck of cards for being a joker. I hate pack mentality.

342

Had a poo in a police station toilet but it wouldn't flush. I've completely lost faith in the cistern.

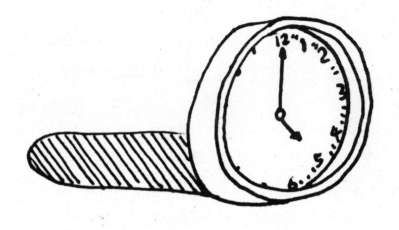

5 O'CLOCK SHADOW

343

I like all my insects to be exactly the same height. Zero taller ants.

344

I've just started a new job hunting vampires. I'm out for the Count.

345

I was on the train chatting up this girl when, somewhere between Hatfield and Knebworth, she suddenly got off! Thought I was Welwyn.

346

My hairdresser accidentally dyed my hair jet black and refused to give me a refund. It's not fair.

347

I was making pancakes for lunch when I looked at the clock and realised it was 4pm already. Really crêpt up on me.

BORED GAME

348

I used to brush my turkey with seasoning at work . . . Baste at home now.

349

I was being interviewed on GMTV and the presenter asked, 'Is that a flan?' I said, 'No, it's a quiche, Lorraine.'

350

Went to a discount clothing store.
All the staff had big moustaches
and were on exactly the same
wage. I realised I was in TK Marx.

ELDERFLOWER

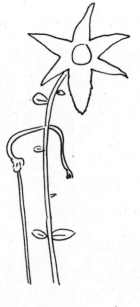

351

I was watching the football team
training, when I noticed all the lads
had their phones on silent. Must've
been the quiet coach.

352

Heard about the magician who put his assistant in a steam room? Went horribly wrong. Ended up sauna in half.

353

For a change, I used Lenor in my laundry. I was outside my Comfort zone.

354

I took my new girlfriend on a date to an owl sanctuary. That turned a few heads.

355

Just broke up with a jigsaw. Something was missing.

356

Captain Kirk's spaceship has been repossessed. He forgot to send his Chekov.

357

Witnessed a group of sheep in a nightclub have a fight with a bunch of lightbulbs. It was Ewe V. Lighting.

358

Took a group of tourists on a really short sightseeing trip to see some legendary creatures of Crete. It was a minor tour.

359

My new ID card is shaped like a shrimp. It's the prawn identity.

360
Got woken up by a rowdy gang drinking hot milky drinks with traffic cones on their heads. Bloody alchohorlicks.

361
Ordered some fries online. Chip off the ol' blog.

OPEN MIC

DANDELION

362

Accidentally trod in my girlfriend's dad's cement. Didn't leave a good impression.

363

My friend spilt curry all down my top. 'Oops, there goes my korma,' he said. That's putting it mildly.

364

I falsely accused my little brother of stealing my Michael Jackson LP. My bad.

365

Got a tattoo of Jesus Christ on my wrist. I shouldn't have used the Lord's name in vein.

366

Some tablets get bad press.

367

Just quit my job at pest control. My boss was fuming.

368

I make sure all my cupboard doors are shut when I have visitors. I'm shelf-conscious.

FLY SWOT

369

Supposed to be going on a balloon ride, but it's all up in the air at the moment.

370

My mate has just bought a pub. I want inn.

371

I was thinking about getting a marble sculpture of my face. But I shouldn't get a head of myself.

372

Just got back from the Amazon, converting the natives to Christianity. Was a right mission.

373

Just found out I'm gonna be a father: I passed my priest exam.

374

To all the people dressing up as sharks: it's wearing fin.

375

Ever since I removed the shell from my snail, it's started feeling sluggish.

376

Saw a tractor, a forklift and a bulldozer performing. The tractor and forklift were good, but the bulldozer brought the house down.

377

Shouldn't have sent my donkey tightrope walking. My ass is on the line.

 NO ENTRY

378

Peroxide. Can't say fairer than that.

379

Went to see two psychiatrists at the same time. Woke up with a massive headache. You should never mix your shrinks.

380

I'm really worried that I might have hypochondria.

381

Told Frank Spencer his name was written in the Hebrew Bible and he believed me! Psalm mothers do 'ave 'em.

382

It looks like my 'Battleships' joke has already been done. Damn, I missed the boat on that one.

383

I use a parsnip to remember what page I'm on. That's a turnip for the books.

SVEN DIAGRAM

BULLET POINT

384
Did a gig in Venice. Nice to have an audience of genuine punters.

385
Got deported to the USA. I was in a state when I got there.

386
Broke a dollar. It made cents.

387

I won *Big* in Vegas! Shame I don't own a DVD player. I'm not that keen on Tom Hanks anyway.

388

My phone kept shouting, 'I AM serious, and don't call me Shirley!' I had it in *Airplane!* mode.

POLITE NOTICE

389

A bunch of youths have been trying to teach me how to talk 'street', but my heart's not innit.

390

A French hen asked me to babysit for her, but I've got an œuf to worry about.

391

Thought I'd try and sneak a rugby ball through the barrier at customs. Worth a try.

392

How many times has Dracula wandered off by himself? I've lost Count.

393

Shouldn't have done my Moses
joke, always divides the room.

394

My friend had a bunch of head lice
in his eyebrow. I said, 'What's going
on there?' He said, 'Oh, they're just
out on the lash.'

SCOOBY DIVING

395

I like to ride my bythicle. I'm a cyclisp.

VANESSA FELTS

396

Saw a couple of Jpegs having an argument the other day. It was a lovers' tif.

397

Entered a painters and decorators costume competition. I was the overall winner.

398

I woo ladies using Sun-Pat peanut butter. Smooth.

399

I've already told the waiter I don't want Parmesan. He's starting to grate on me.

400

This girl wants me to meet her at the entrance to a football stadium. It's not really my stile.

401

My mother keeps hesitating when deciding what to eat. She's going through the menu-pause.

HIGH IN TENT SETTEE

402

Dressed my car up like a melancholy, melodramatic, angsty teenager. I hope it passes its emo-t.

BAND WAGON

403

Whenever I play away from home, I always come third. I guess it comes with the tertiary.

404

I live in my landlady's head, but I forgot to pay last month's rent. I'm in 'er ears.

405

I got quite far in the old lady fancy dress tournament, but didn't make the gran final.

SUSPICIOUS MINDS

406

I've been told I should pursue my psychic abilities, but I'm in two minds.

407

I was trying to get backstage at a power tools gig, but the bouncer stopped me. I said, 'It's OK, I know the drill.'

408

My TV keeps winking at me. I think it's on the blink.

409

My ex-wife took me to court about a dispute over who owned our apple pies. She got custardy.

410

I'm selling the smell of flowers. 50p per fume.

411

A fortune teller told me that one day I would receive raffles, cakes, coconut shies and Morris dancers. I'm just going to have to accept my fête.

SPIRIT LEVEL

412

Woke up to find a luminous wooden hut at the bottom of my garden. Hope someone can shed some light on it.

413

Aggragaphobia: fear of losing on away goals.

WIND-UP MERCHANT

414

Had a job as a luggage handler, but I packed it in.

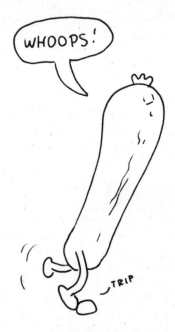

CUMBERSOME SAUSAGE

415

Single lanes are the best roads for driving on. There's no two ways about it.

416

Did a gig at a Greek wedding. Smashed it.

417

They're telling me my bag has been found in lost luggage, but I don't think that's the case.

NOT MY CUP OF TEA

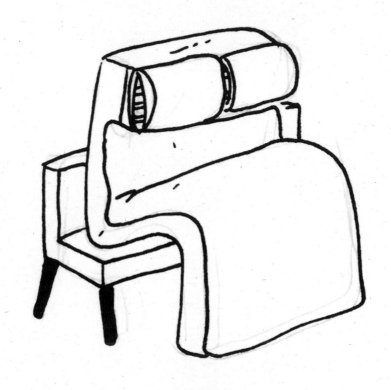

BEDSIT

418

I drove past a political rally earlier, but didn't see much. I'm going back to have a proper gander.

FLUKEY

419

I set up two pyromaniacs on a blind date. They're getting on like a house on fire.

420

I keep throwing a Frisbee at my dog's head. I've got really bad hound-eye coordination.

421

I come from a mixed-race family. My dad was in the hurdles, my mother ran in the 400-metre relay.

422

The idea of a hippie shoving his hair down my throat fills me with dread.

423

My dog's paws are huge. Really long gap between his woofs.

FALSE TEETH

424

A man has been arrested for breaking into a constable's kitchen and making a roast with far too much seasoning. He was wasting police thyme.

425

I got a job as a pantomime horse. They wanted me to switch ends, but I thought, I'll quit while I'm a head.

426

I was trying to think what the French word for 'white' was, but my mind went blanc.

427

I studied Locksmithery at Yale.

428

Self-cannibalism: some people are so full of themselves.

429

A stunt-double friend of mine has just got a job playing Indiana Jones's saliva. He's the spit of Harrison Ford.

IPOD

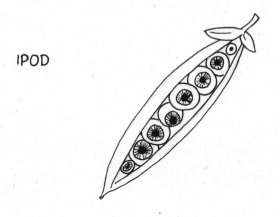

430

Tried to abbreviate the word 'number' to a one-character symbol. Made a hash of it.

POLLEN COUNT

431

I tried to get a female sheep from a vending machine, but it was out of ewes.

432

My gran is having surgery to make her more trendy and fashionable. It's a hip operation.

433

I don't mind it when people tell me I'm paranoid to my face. It's when they say I'm paranoid behind my back that really makes me cross!

434

I was Yogi's best man, but then I lost my bear rings.

435

Heard about the crew of sultanas that entered a boat race? They lost to some strong currants.

436

Went to Tesco to find a man running around with his hand in a naughty glove puppet. It was supermarket Sweep.

RETRACTABLE PEN

THE CHEQUE IS IN THE POST

437

How am I going to sell all this
Chinese gangster paraphernalia? I
might try ads.

438

. . . and that concludes my lecture on
vacuum cleaners, so let's press on.

439
The 8th dwarf was lesser gnome.

440
When eating German bangers and mash, I always eat the potato first. Save the wurst till last.

441
My girlfriend had a go at me for marinating chicken, skewering it and sticking it on a grill. Sheesh.

442
Cadbury announce a new chocolate bar that will give the economy a much-needed boost.

AWKWARD

443
I can't believe the annual air show is here again. It's flown by.

444
He uses acne cream, because it doesn't work. What an Oxy moron.

445
Wait till you hear my
procrastination joke . . .

446
Put a stuffed bear in the oven. Ted
baker.

447

My friend thinks I'm high maintenance. Whenever I meet him for a pint, he says, 'Hi, mate, Tennent's?.'

448

Crushing up almonds into a paste and eating them before I go to bed really helps me sleep. Ta, marzipan.

CURRANT AFFAIR

449

I covered my DVD collection with photos of Jennifer Aniston, David Schwimmer and Courtney Cox. I wanted it to look like I had friends.

450

I convinced two identical siblings that they could walk in different directions. Conned joined twins.

451

My father used to tell me I was really good at holding a grudge. I've never forgiven him for saying that.

452

Anita cut my hair.

453

My parents called my younger brother Tipp-Ex, because he was a mistake.

454

I have a Casio watch that stops working if it's worn by Tom Hanks or Daryl Hannah. It's *Splash*-proof.

455

I ate some Japanese peas covered in mustard. Wasabi? It's a small green vegetable.

456

I'm really good at cooling down hot muffins, but I'm not going to blow my own crumpet.

SINGAPORE

457
Your beetroot soup is reddy.

458
I got a job inscribing the names of movie stars on the Hollywood Walk of Fame. When I saw my own name on there, I knew that I'd made it.

GIRLY KNIGHT

459

Ancient history for dummies: easy BC.

460

Heard the one about the old man who spent his entire life trying to grow carrots on his allotment? He eventually found peas.

461

I received a phone call whilst I was in Malta, but I couldn't answer it because I was in the middle of Mdina.

462

Someone passed on an email from a girl that said 'My mate fancies you.' I thought, that's a bit forward.

463

A crocodile managed to win a court case accusing him of leaving rubbish everywhere. He was a litigator.

FILE EXTENSION

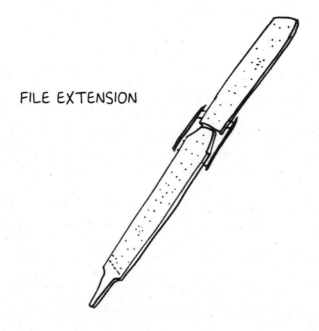

464

A feral rodent has been accused of leaving rubbish everywhere. It couldn't read the charges it was given because it was a litter rat.

465

A hotel developer said he was going to build one more hotel complex. I said, 'OK, but that's the last resort.'

466

I received a cucumber and garlic yoghurt for my birthday. Tzatziki what I wanted.

467

No, thanks. I'm not drying up dishes anymore. I'm teatotowel.

468

I went out for dinner where every meal was either striped or spotted. It was a tie restaurant.

469
My mate Dave always helps me plug in my instruments just before I go on stage. He's a sound guy.

470
I ate the 'recently deceased' section of a newspaper. It was a bit chewy.

471
I asked a tailor to come round and shorten my trousers, but he didn't turn up.

472
Persuading a raisin that it is a sultana: con currant.

473

Wish I hadn't bought a house in Grimsby. Neighbours from Hull.

474

My car is powered by Indian headscarves. It's a turban engine.

475

Ever since I added an extra floor to my bungalow, people are giving me stares.

476

Got told off by my dad for leaving his car running. He started it.

477

My wife buys stockings that are really cheap. I thought, that's a bit tight.

478

People wonder why I shoplift board games based on world domination. It's because I'm a bit of a Risk taker.

479

I suddenly decided to sort all my playing cards into pairs. It was a snap decision.

JUST LANDED A MASSIVE ROLL IN HOLLYWOOD

480

Went to a shop that sold nothing but pins and notice boards. It was a bit tacky.

481

I asked the barman for some Belgian beer, but there was none Leffe.

IRRELEPHANT

482

Sponges are so self-absorbed.

483

Antimatter is neither here nor there.

484

A plumber turned up at my house.
'CHAAARGE!' he shouted.
I replied, 'No need for that.'
He said, 'Sorry, call out charge.'

485

It took the Spanish man ages to tell me he didn't know. Long time no sé.

SATSUMO

486

I was trying to find my way out of the church after attending the Christmas service. Luckily there was a mass exit.

HORSE FLY

487

Went shopping for a jack-in-the-box, but nothing jumped out at me.

488

Buddhist law-enforcement officers are calmer police.

489

I covered my lounge in a fizzy red-coloured soft drink. Tizer room together.

PRIVILEGED BACKGROUND

490

Watched a gruesome film about people inhaling tobacco through their nose. It was a snuff movie.

PHONE CHARGED

491

I worked in a bakery, but there were too many cooks. I felt cake tin.

492

Ian Astbury, Billy Duffy, John Tempesta and Chris Wyse have just added me on Twitter. I've got a Cult following.

493

I asked my friend how she picks up men in a solarium. She went off on a tan gent.

494

I went on a romantic package holiday with a group of over-50s vampires. It was the Twilight Saga.

495

I amost got attacked by a minotaur with a speech impediment. It was a near myth.

496

Clumsy marimba delivery men bring bad vibes.

497

I investigated The Mystery of the Missing Oyster. It was an open-and-shut case.

498

I went to an Oriental restaurant, but everything on the menu came with teabags. It was Typhoo'ed.

SALAD DRESSING

499

My mate kept throwing rubbish all over the floor – it was hilarious. I guess you had to have bin there.

Y KNOT

500

If you're allergic to fibre, you must constantly be wondering what might have bean.

501

Hospitals in the impoverished areas of 1980s New York used ghetto plasters.

CAT WALK

502

How many in-jokes does it take to change a light bulb? Four! LOL.

503

My actor friend threw his family out of his house and moved his stunt double in. I don't know how he can live with himself.

504

I kept telling people to be quiet, but I didn't mean it. I just wanted to look important. Pretend shush.

505

If one pizza delivery company closes down, they all close down. It's the Domino's effect.

506

I rented out my potty to a toddler.
It was a toy let.

507

My Peter Pan joke never gets old.

FORTIFIED WINE

508

My paper airplane almost hit the
teacher. Near miss.

HONEYMOON

509

I missed a documentary about tomato sauce, but luckily I managed to watch it on ketchup.

510

Had a secret relationship with the Norse god of trickery. It was a Loki affair.

511

This guy put his hand in a blender and swallowed it. I don't understand it as I don't drink myself.

512

I don't think a pea would make good tofu, but a bean curd.

513

Tried to play the piano with a slice of pork, but it kept getting stuck to the keys. Chop sticks.

514

I got a Valentine's card from a girl saying 'Guess who?' I don't like women who play games . . . especially Guess Who?™

515

Bisquits: cookies that give up easily.

516

I gave my girlfriend a pair of beige vintage '80s trousers. I didn't say who they were from, but chinos . . .

517

I was lonely and wanted some company, so I changed my name to Darren Walsh Ltd.

518

I've started doing comedy in a chicken coop. That'll ROFL some feathers.

519

Abacus factories: it's what's on the inside that counts.

CRACKED PEPPER

520

My friend didn't want anyone knowing he was buried, so he changed his name by deep hole.

521

In Korean restaurants, they call their dogs Marmite, because you either love them or ate them.

BAD STOMACH

522

My mate ordered garlic bread with a raw turnip on it. He's always had this weird side to him.

523

Caught my mate listening to Beethoven. Classic!

524

'That's all that comes with the snooker table I'm afraid,' claimed the shop assistant. I said, 'Yeah, and the rest . . .'

525

Ballerinas: you've got to keep them on their toes.

526

I tried it on with my comedy partner the other day: a pantomime horse costume.

BED LAMB

527

Got a shirty email from the dry cleaners.

528

Went to a nightclub called Suitcase. It was packed.

529

I haven't brushed my teeth in ages. Everyone is avoiding me like the plaque.

530

My girlfriend keeps putting pressure on me to rearrange the sitting-room furniture, but she can only push me sofa . . .

531

Lost touch with my old bobsleigh team. Shouldn't have let friendships slide.

532

Weak lager is not one of my strong pints.

533

They're making a new horror movie
in Russia about politicians that
turn into savage creatures if you
feed them after midnight. Kremlins.

534

I read that Pluto got demoted.
Unbelievable. You couldn't planet.

535

I can't find the Great Bear either,
if it's any constellation . . .

536

People with dermatitis really grate
on me.

ANIMOSCITY

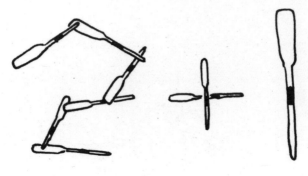

AWESOME

537
Someone drew a treasure map all over me. I'm parched.

538
I chat up women by defrosting their frozen cars. I'm a woman icer.

539
My wife gave birth to a pack of cards. I guess we're just going to have to deal with it.

TUNA STAKE

540

I've put money into the first letter of every sentence. It's a capital investment.

541

What do you call an American president loaded with vitamin C? Berocca Bama.

CALAMAORI

542

I let all my chickens escape!
Somehow I'm going to have to
recoup my losses . . .

543

Went on a date with this girl, but
she said she had to go off. It was a
sell-by date.

544

I made a pair of binoculars out
of fish fingers. I wanted to get a
Birds Eye view.

545

I've met an old flame at college.
We've got History.

546

My wife's worried that our son is hanging out with too many cooks, spoiling broth. I said, 'Don't worry, it's just a phrase he's going through.'

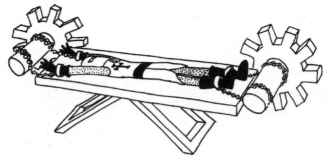

LONG KNIGHT

547

If you think I'm swell, you should meet my Auntie Histamine.

548

Marcel Marceau tried to steal my rope. I told him it was mime.

549

OK, you've got to quickly seal that airtight door before the second one opens. No pressure.

550

I have no time for flatfish. I'm plaicist.

551

I never wanted to ride in the back of a police car. I just got pushed into it.

HELLO?

THIS WAY UP

PHONE BOX

552

We all dressed up in bog roll on that stag do. Kept getting ripped off by the locals.

553

I did a gig at an astronomers' conference. Apparently they only like observational humour.

554

Inland Revenue are confiscating my notice board. Apparently, I didn't have any tacks for it.

555

There's a bakery opening a chain of stores in the ghetto. It's a Ginsters paradise.

556

Tried to make a house out of a nun's hat, but it was uninhabitable.

557

I like my women how I like my tea. To be builders.

TV PILOT

558

I asked the waiter for some hummus, he said, 'Sorry, we only have sushi.' I said, 'CHICK PEAS . . .'

SALMAN RUSHDIE

559

My mate rents out his ego.
He's got a hire opinion of himself.

560

Bokbokbokbook: Facebook for
chickens.

561

On your marks . . . Go! Too soon?

RINGWORM

562

I swapped a portion of thick-cut chips for some fries. Cost me a wedge.

563

People wonder why I invested money in a cathedral. I'm in it for the long hall.

564

As a financial advisor I get to meet a lot of women, but after a while they seem to lose interest.

565

My DJ friend uses cherry-flavoured throat lozenges to hammer in nails. He likes banging Tunes.

566

My girlfriend asked, 'Are you still perving over men's magazines?' I thought, that's a loaded question.

WEEK NIGHT

567

Embarrister: the shame of being a solicitor.

568

I applied to the government for a loan to develop my floppy hair. It was a Hugh grant.

569

Corpoliticallyrect ← Politically in correct.

570

After a heavy night drinking, I like to get brunch in the capital of Lower Saxony. It's Hanover food.

SLOPPY SECONDS

571

I hate giving my mate a lift. He's always like, 'Can we change the music to something more classical?' Bloody Bach seat drivers.

572

My mate keeps losing his temper whenever his boat drifts off. He needs anchor management.

573

Gran father: when your dad dresses up as an old woman.

574

Lending people turf at appallingly high interest rates: lawn sharks.

575

The art of being tall without anyone noticing: subtall.

576

I just painted my clothes stand. I'll give it another coat tomorrow.

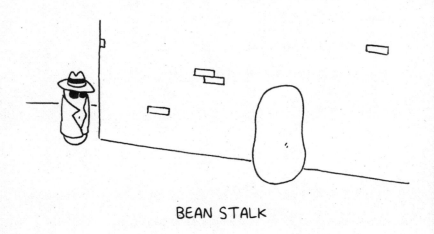

BEAN STALK

577

Someone made my rectangular swimming pool square shaped. Took my breadth away.

MAJOR STEAKHOLDER

578

I went to see David Hasselhoff having a kidney removed. It was open Mike Knight.

579

Told my gran she had bad posture. She got the hump.

580

I should stop mentioning that I hate forklift trucks. People pick up on these things.

581

I took out an insurance policy for my nails, but there was a break claws.

582

I quit my job as a painter and decorator. It got too emulsional.

583

I've got a date with a girl from the sewing machine factory. I don't know her well, but she seams nice.

584

I was feeling a bit depressed, so I picked up a crate of vodka using a forklift truck. That raised my spirits.

585

My nan said that if I did her garden I could have a go on her Stannah stair lift. I said, 'I'll take you up on that.'

GAP YEAR

586

I came out of the sunbed with a pink head, a yellow torso and brown legs. It was a neapoli-tan.

587

If a rooster throws a bachelor party, what does the hen do?

588

My friend can hold a boiling hot cup of tea in the palm of his hand. It's saucery.

589

I went into a tailor's shop but they were too preoccupied to notice I was there. I said, 'A-hem!'

SERIOUS ISSHOES

BLIND DATE

590

For their school science project, the girls at the convent built a giant catapult. They're going to use it as a nun chucka.

591

I got to play a lead part in *Friends*. I'm Rach beyond my wildest dreams.

592

I got invited to a barbecue by a TV survival instructor, but I said no. I can't bear grills.

593

I bought Michael Jackson's last album. It's not *Bad*.

594

Lady MacGyver: a resourceful 11th-century Anglo-Saxon noblewoman who prefers non-violent resolutions using everyday materials she finds at hand.

595

I asked my tennis coach for some serving suggestions. He said, 'Why not try slicing up bits of strawberries in your cornflakes?'

FIRE EXIT

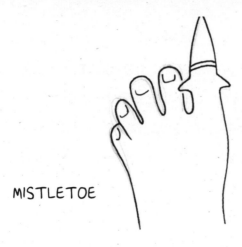

MISTLETOE

596

I manage all Dracula's bookings. I work in a Count Management.

597

I tried to join an extreme anti-science religious group, but they said there was no space.

598

After a stressful day at work I eat a jellyfish. Need a clear head.

599

I walked into a pub and said to the barman, 'Do you do venue hire?'
He said, 'We're on top of a hill, what more do you want?'

600

Put my archery video on YouTube. Only got 3 hits.

601

I was thinking about building only one stronghold, but I'm having second forts.

602

Odeon cinemas have announced Walkers as their new sponsor. Films will feature crisp images.

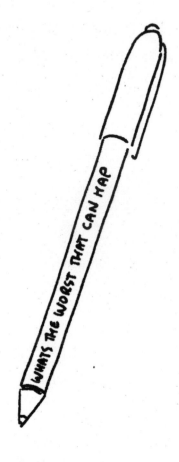

WHAT'S THE WORST THAT CAN HAPPEN?

603

The compère introduced me by saying I was made entirely of Lego. I hate being built up like that.

PHEREMONES

604

My friend Noel is obsessed with leaking conspiracy theories. We call him Grassy Noel.

605

I told one of my pupils to do his tie up, so he put it round his waist, turned round and pulled his trousers down. Smart arse.

606

Trying to convince drivers to cut down on petrol. It's a bit of emission.

STAND IN KNIFE

607

The House of Commons couldn't decide what type of cupboard to put in their bathroom, so they had a cabinet meeting.

608

London's cafés are a good place two meat and veg.

609

Speedy Gonzales has started a new job as a forklift driver. He's picking things up quite quickly.

610

What do you call a vegetable that does Kung Fu? Brock Lee.

611

I'm putting on a gig for a mountain rescue charity. It's difficult to pick acts.

CHAPSTICK

612

Visited a place called Boil. It's a nice spot.

613

The guy that works at the bank doesn't talk much. He's a bit of a loaner.

614

I drank my window. It was the only thing that would take the pane away.

615

My maths pupils turned my minus sign into a plus sign. They've crossed the line this time.

BULLDOZER

616

I asked my dog who his favourite classical composer was. He said Bach.

617

Some people like to dress up as cookers, but I'm not a fan oven.

618

I've opened a new restaurant specialising in edible nocturnal birds. It's owl you can eat.

619

I accidentally raised your child. Sorry, didn't mean to bring him up . .

HEBREW

620

The post office doesn't know where to deliver my magazine. Someone needs to address the issue."

CURED HAM

621

Typed the word 'disabled' into my computer, but it said the password was invalid.

622

My mother told me to look after her parking tickets. Fine with me.

623

Caught an Italian trying to steal my bread. I said, 'Focaccia doing that again . . .'

624

I tried to make a korma, but I ended up with the hottest curry imaginable. Epic phaal.

625

Using a bottle of anti-dandruff shampoo works much better as a snooker cue. Head & Shoulders above the rest.

626

Went shopping for muggers but nothing grabbed me.

627

I imprisoned a Samurai Warrior
in a sheep's enclosure. The pen is
mightier than the sword.

628

Right, that's it. No more 'connect
the dots' puzzles. I have to draw
the line somewhere.

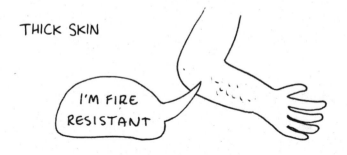

THICK SKIN

I'M FIRE
RESISTANT

629

America has created a new
overprotective territory called Au
Pair. It's a nanny state.

630

I'm very easily distrac

GRRRRRRR!

AGGRESSIVE MANOR

631

That's a nice nightie ← Compliment
slip.

632

My brother keeps wearing all my
old clothes from when I was a boy.
He's always trying to be little me.

633

My girlfriend said I should be more romantic, so I put on a centurion's helmet and attached myself to her neck.

634

The Michelin Man asked me to carry him across a floor of broken glass, but I'm worried I might let him down.

I JUST CAN'T SEEM TO GET OUT OF BED IN THE MORNINGS...

DEPRESSED BUTTON

635

My mate is half Irish, half Chinese.
He's Cork-Asian.

636

Went to a strippers club once.
It was great – there was enough
wallpaper for everyone.

637

Wool farm closed down due to
shear volume of complaints.

638

Some people think it's bad taste
to collect body parts from various
areas of India, but I've been given
the Goa head.

MOCK TUDOR

639

All I can think about is bacon-
flavoured crisps. My mind is
frazzled.

640

My girlfriend discovered a secret
book of cows under my mattress.
It wasn't the main reason we broke
up, but it was the cattle list.

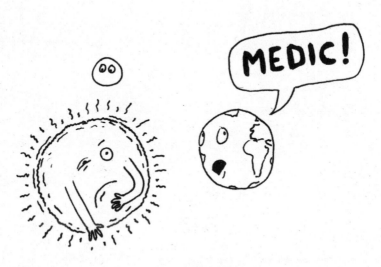

SUNSTROKE

RONSEAL

641

Could someone tell me how to avoid getting mugged? Cos I'm in the dark here.

642

Cod liver is good for your joints. It's a fish oil.

643

Tried to write the word 'epileptic' in a crossword. Didn't fit.

644
I ate a polo, whole.

645
Want to be a plastic surgeon? Go to collagen get a degree.

646
My wrists smell nice. I use cuff Lynx.

647
Went on a date with a chicken. All she talked about was her eggs.

648
'Originality is undetected plagiarism.' – Darren Walsh.

649

This bloke asked me if I wanted to swap dogs, but I think he had an old terrier motive.

650

'Why have you started talking like a cat?'
'Look, just hear meow . . .'

INTELLIGERBIL

651
My boss asked me if he could have a quiet word. I whispered, 'Yes . . .'

652
The girl from the tanning salon has started speaking Mandarin. Always thought she was a little orange.

BUNNY BOILER

HUMAN BEATBOX

I'VE GOT ALL YOUR ALBUMS...

CEILING FAN

653

I had a yoghurt with a small portion of curried owls. Müller g'tawny.

654

Saw a sign at the zoo that said 'Do not feed the monkey chocolate' but I thought I'd give it a whirl anyway.

655

I think it's time I laid that swearing joke Tourette's.

656

A pet shop are having a closing-down sale. It's a dead giveaway.

657

I'm rubbish with names. That's why I called both my kids Brian.

SABRE TOOTH

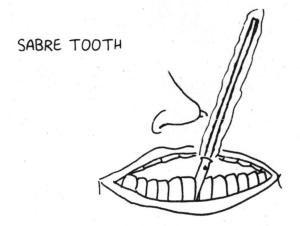

658

My mum's acting weird lately —
keeps getting hot flushes and
raiding my piggy bank. She's going
through the change.

POACHED EGG

659

Bought a pack of burger baps,
hoping that at least one of them
would give me an idea for a joke,
but no bun in ten did.

660

My South American friend hunts huge mammals in the canals of Italy, using a harpoon. He's a Venice whaler.

661

Lions in elevators again? There's going to be an uproar.

662

My mate has an addiction to dressing up like a nun. He's stealing to pay for his habit.

663

Bought some halal meat, labelled as normal meat. It was a blessing in disguise.

664
Aren't all CDs metal albums?

665
Went to a fish and chip shop, but they had no fish! Just lots of perfectly cooked chips. Turned out it was an efficient chip shop.

666
My parents are Jen and Eric. They're generic names.

667
My mate Ray Diation is a bit much sometimes, but he's alright in small doses.

668
Full-time crime doesn't PAYE.

669
I just sprayed my suit with anti-chicken spray. It's impeccable.

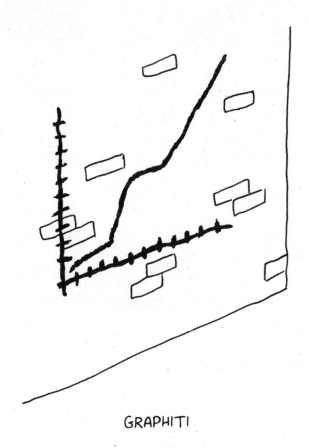

GRAPHITI

FACE DOWN

670

Went to a rap concert, but it was Tupac'd.

671

Took my daughter to a maze, because I thought it would be fun. Then I lost Faith.

THE TABLES HAVE TURNED

672

I want to speed date, but there is no quick figs.

673

I was going to quit my karate lessons. Luckily I came to my senseis.

674

Terrible audience at Brad and Angelina's wedding. They were the Pitts.

675

At first, I wasn't sure what kind of bird I had, until it started talking. Then it became a parrot.

676

I thought it was my moth that kept singing annoying opera, but it was m'damn butterfly.

PRESSURE COOKER

677

'Meet my sister, she's an emergency worker too.'
'Yeah, I can see the resambulance.'

BABY SHOWER

678
It's OK to steal nuts as long as they don't cashew.

679
The stewardess asked me if I wanted to stand. I said, 'It's OK, aisle seat.'

680
All my peers are more driven than I am. They have their own chauffeurs.

681

Someone stole an entire genre of my DVD collection. Ah well, no dramas.

682

'Do you want me to row to the left or right?'
'Either oar.'

CAST IRON

683

I told a shepherd to put me in a pen but I'm still not in it. He must not have herd me.

684

I baked some foundation and gave it to my girlfriend. She is now cake tin make-up.

685

Looks like I'm going to have to ask my geeky Spanish classmate for help with my homework again. Back to square Juan.

686

I'm tired of waiting for Amber. She seems to be forever getting ready.

FRIENDLY FIRE

687

What's a sarcastic cow's favourite motorbike? Kawasaki.

688

Even when my head hits the pillow, I'm still thinking of puns. Always on the case.

TO BE HONEST, I DON'T THINK YOU'RE SMART ENOUGH TO GET THIS JOKE

CANDID CAMERA

689

My boss is always saying, 'You don't have to be mad to work here, but it helps!' He's office head.

DIMMER SWITCH

690

My rooster woke me up an hour late. Forgot to put the clucks forward.

691

If you wanna get Rich quick, call him.

692

I put fabric softener all over my ice cream. I just needed some Comfort food.

693

This girl told me her daddy issues. How awful. I'm glad my dad isn't shoes.

JUNGLE BOOGIE

694

I tried to make a samurai out of wax, but I forgot m'damn two swords.

695

The Incredible Hulk has been hired to change several bus routes in London. He's pulling out all the stops.

696

Superman is running out of arch-enemies. He's on his last Lex.

697

I installed some software on my computer, selected English, then clicked 'Finish'. Can't read a thing.

698

Met an actor who said he was in *Hollyoaks* for 4 years then *Casualty* for 5 years. I can't believe *Hollyoaks* did that to him.

QUICK TURNOVER

THE LION'S CHER

699

I went into an estate agents and they offered me an instant coffee, but I just wanted a proper tea.

700

I sold a set of door knobs to a Weight Watchers class. They love handles.

701

Applied to the council for a cage, water-bottle and wheel. They said I wasn't eligerbil.

702

I preferred the Wombles when they were more underground.

703

'Oh yeah, sure, my boat can hold all those animals.' Noah'sark-astic.

704

Man walks into a baa. The sheep says, 'Do you mind? I'm still talking.'

SYMPATHY VOTE

705

Doctors have discovered a lump of ice cream in my brain. Luckily it's not serious. It's benign. Benign Jerry's.

706

I met my girlfriend reading her name in the small print of a contract. She's a catch.

707

I owe all my success to my wife. Should never have signed that prenup.

708

Call me lazy, but

709

Saw a congregation of probiotic yoghurts worshipping a Himalayan cow. It was a yak cult.

DRUGS WEARING OFF

710

My friend said, 'I've got a photo of you on my Piano.' I had no idea pianos could take photos.

711

Digging for fossils is a mammoth tusk.

LAST TANGO IN PARIS

712

I let Macaulay Culkin borrow my *Simpsons* doll. It was a Homer loan.

713

I mistook a group of floating beacons for fish. School/Buoy error.

714

My American friend keeps mentioning his forefathers. (He had a troubled childhood.)

715

My teacher asked me to choose my favourite body part, so I picked my nose.

716
Saw a clown jogging whilst eating chocolate cereal. Coco puffs.

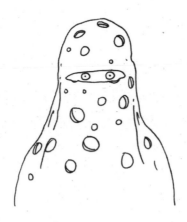

CHEESE BURQA

717
My mate Ian is half Indian.

718
An American told me I was no bigger than his dog. I don't like being critter-sized.

IT WENT UP YOUR SLEEVE

SMARTPHONE

719

There's a rumour going round that residents of African islands murder tourists. It's just Mauritius.

720

This bloke told me the ninth Egyptian king was French. I thought, Pharaoh Neuf.

721

Went to the doctor, said I might
have rumourtism. He said, 'Yeah, I
heard someone say that . . .'

722

I've lost 6 pounds since going to
the gym. Hopefully someone will
hand it in at reception.

FIREPLACE

723

Burt Reynolds was selling unsmoked bacon in Tel Aviv, but he went smokey and they banned it.

724

Thought I'd got away with farting on an Irish budget airline, but air lingers.

725

My friend peeled a banana, split it down the middle, shoved it into my face and ran off. I hate it when people dessert me like that.

726

Bought a Dracula-themed clock. Every second Counts.

727

I got asked to build a dining area for an army barracks. Made a big mess.

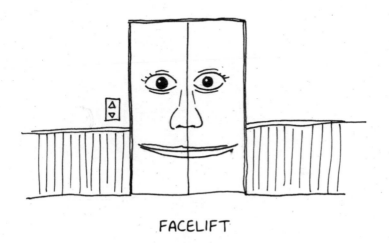

FACELIFT

728

A Sherpa ripped my map. He said, 'I tore guide.'

729

I met a guy who thought he was a vacuum cleaner. He got suctioned.

CAGEY BEE

730

Latvia's beaches are quite rocky, but some of the neighbouring countries Estonia.

BOILED KETTLE

731

Read a book on milk. The last chapter was semi-skimmed.

732

An android told me that I made his brains fall out. Must've had a chip on his shoulder.

733

Broke down on the motorway and pulled over onto the cold shoulder. It's like the hard shoulder, except everyone ignores you . . .

THE CENTRE OF ATTENTION

734

I told my mate he should give up on his dream of being a dentist. He couldn't handle the tooth.

735

My mate reckons we should all dress up as chestnuts. I conker.

736

I named my horse Sarah and sang her love songs in a horse voice. It was nice when Sarah neighed me back.

737

Bought a tub of I Can't Believe It's Not Homer. Turned out it was Marge.

MAN CRUSH

738

Note to shelf: 'Dear shelf,'

739

I bought a calendar at the airport shop featuring the captains of Bahamas Air, Air Jamaica and Haïti Ambassador Airlines. Pilots of the Caribbean.

740

I asked an anaesthesiologist if she wanted to go for a drink and she said yes. S'date.

741

I was furious at my girlfriend for using our car to measure distances at thoroughbred horse races, but I can't stay mad at her furlong.

TYRES SLASHED

STAFF ANNOUNCEMENT

742

Someone dumped a lorryful of mannequins on my front lawn. Van dolls.

743

Because of last year's damaged goods, Barack Obama is delivering gifts this Christmas. It's unpressiedented.

744

My mate always offers pregnant women his seat. He's ultra sound.

745

My grandad got buried under a hen coop. Chicks dig him.

746

My cat fell in the liquidiser. Pour cat.

WIFE BEATER

747

I promised I'd hand-deliver my dog's Christmas present, but I might have to post bone.

748

I thought I could postpone my vasectomy, but there's a cut-off date.

COCONUT SHY

749

Went to a Gabrielle concert.
Wasn't a patch on her in the '80s.

750

Some people say investment
bankers don't appreciate their job,
but I met one who said every day is
a bonus.

751

If you want to open an Arnold
Schwarzenegger movie on your
Mac, it's Cmd+O.

752

Sleeping pills don't work if you wake
them up.

753

Just got temporary a job at a hairdressers. Thinking about perm.

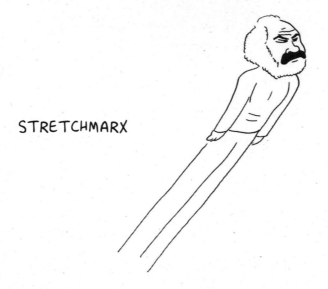

STRETCHMARX

754

I rented out a guy's anxieties.
It was the lease of his worries.

755

I used to play a fruit machine with both arms, but one arm banned it.

756

Just one lumberjack for me,
thanks. I'm trying to cut down.

757

My mother once told me to never
marry a traffic warden. Fine.

758

Can't stop eating boats, they're
really moorish.

CALL TO ARMS

MAN SIGHS TISSUE

759

Went on an Internet date dressed as Colonel Gaddafi. Didn't go that well. Turned out she wanted a Libran.

760

I got dumped by a waitress just because I worked at environmental health. I'm going to see her one last time . . . I need closure.

EARLY DOORS

761

I think they should make air-freshener in jasmine and elderflower. That's my two scents.

762

I thought I saw a lettuce, a red onion and a cherry tomato doing a striptease. Turned out it was just a salad dressing.

MOUNT SAINT BERNARD

763

Whenever you sign a contract with a cat, watch out for the get-out claws.

764

My friend sold me a bunch of gardening implements really cheap. Mate's rakes.

765

The BNPP (British National Plumbers Party): goes against just about every sink I believe in.

766

I was playing hide-and-seek with a bunch of deer, when I accidentally sneezed. That gave the game away.

SAFE HANDS

767

I strangled a greengrocer dressed as Picasso. It was an arty choke.

768

Tried to throw a donkey into a waterhole. Didn't go down well.

769

My friend said he'd go to any lengths to cure his skin condition. I hope he doesn't do anything rash.

770

Whilst giving a sermon, the vicar shouted, 'If your name's Peter, clear off!' It was a good service, but it petered out towards the end.

771

My friend was distraught that he missed his therapy session for self-harming. I said, 'Don't beat yourself up about it.'

FORK PROVOKING

772

Found a packet of polos in the loft, mint condition.

773

My friend does stand-up comedy with his back to the crowd. Nothing faces him.

HEN KNIGHT

774

I like my women how I like my beer: to be named Becks.

MOODY

775

Heard the one about the depressed satchel? Bit of a sad case.

776

People who send written protests against penalty fares . . . I don't see the appeal.

FOREHEAD

777

Went to a party in a Medieval castle. It was rammed.

CZECH POINT

778

Man found not guilty of stealing Microsoft Office software: he's got away with Words.

779

Was going to do my omelette joke, but I'm not going to whisk it.

CROISSANT

780

Woke up with a numb arm wearing a clown costume. Must've slept on it funny.

781

Sumo wrestling in a monastery? Fat chants.

782

I asked the waiter what 'Jacobth Creek Thardonnay' was. He said, 'Sorry, that's the wine lisp.'

783

I convinced someone to go to prison with no pillows. I gave him the hard cell.

784

My teenage nephew has gone to Glastonbury for the first time. He's at that in-between stage.

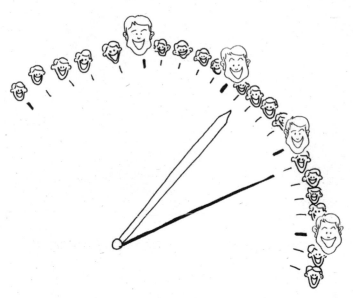

ONE BOURNE EVERY MINUTE

PIZZERIA

785

My friend said he'd let me help out at the water park dolphin show, but I'm not gonna get my hoops up.

786

Took a dog-walking test on an aeroplane. Passed with flying collars.

787

I was going to reunite the 1984 Liverpool squad, but there's no Rush.

788

Tried to sail the English Channel using a thick slice of gammon, but it was a bit too choppy.

789

When she started talking about hummus there was a dip in the conversation.

PLEASE DON'T HURT ME

FRAID EDGE

790

I didn't know how my water purifier worked, but now it's become clear.

791

I refuse to stop believing in Father Christmas. I guess I'm too Santamental.

792

A tourist on the London Dungeon tour asked me to take a photo of him posing next to a guillotine. It didn't look good — I cut his head off.

793

Watching a reality-television programme touring the house of baby Jesus. It's *MTV Cribs*.

LIGHTNING STRIKE

794

I can only remember things from up to 7 days ago. I'm week minded.

795

I had too many parents. They christened me Broth. They were chefs. I was spoilt.

796

Edinburgh's Arthur's Seat: named so after a pensioner left his car at the top.

797

Just looking at my bungee-jumping holiday photos. Ah, it takes me back.

798

Oregano makes up for lost thyme.

799

A market researcher asked me, 'Can I ask you a few questions about the brand of deodorant you use?' I said, 'Sure.'

NO THANKS I'M SAVING MYSELF...

MORAL COMPASS

800

I woke up to find my calendar had Monday missing. Must've been a blank holiday.

801

Hired a bouncy castle. What a massive let-down.

802

Drank a coffee, now I'm full of beans.

803

I employed a personal assistant but she kept shouting, 'I ain't making no coffee, fool.' It was PA Baracus.

CHIP MONK

804

Pretended I was Roger Daltrey.
Who new.

MALE ORDER BRIDE

805

I like my steak how I like to
patronise: well done.

806

Couldn't sleep last night. I kept
thinking about my missing remote.
It was impossible to switch off.

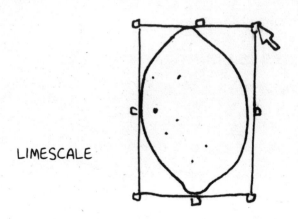

LIMESCALE

807

Got to dig out all these snails from the back of the freezer. It's going to be a long, hard slug.

808

I don't believe in atheism.

809

My mate wanted to drive back to his house drunk. I said, 'Crash at mine.'

810

'That bloke is singing Christmas carols like an owl.'
'Hoo, hymn?'

811

I love making tartar sauce, it just takes ages scraping it off your teeth.

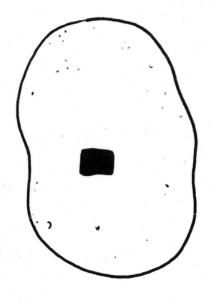

DICTATA

812

I had 2 chicken legs and 6 chicken wings yesterday. Hopefully, after today's operation, I can start to live a normal life again.

CASH POINT

813

I still haven't got the hang of using plural.